ADOPTION

STORIES

Excerpts from
Adoption Books for Adults

Compiled by the co-founder of
ADOPTION TRUTH & TRANSPARENCY
WORLDWIDE NETWORK

ADOPTION STORIES

Excerpts from Adoption Books for Adults

***

co-founder of
ADOPTION TRUTH & TRANSPARENCY WORLDWIDE NETWORK

"If we remain positive and accept what is, if we tend to pay attention to the beauty of the practice but not examine the insides, we will be less likely to give ourselves the benefit of the doubt, and we will forgo the potential beauty of our birth culture and if we forgo the potential of our birth culture, it's harder to see the beauty within ourselves."

~Janine Vance
Americanized '72
A Generation-X Coming of Age (& Identity)
Adoption Story

CONTENTS

Note from the Co-Founder of the
Adoption Truth and Transparency
Worldwide Network

I believe information is power. This writing is intended to empower you. I believe that you deserve to know more than the politicians in the field so that you can approach the discussion with confidence, knowing to the fullest extent possible, your human rights.

As someone who has researched the industry for two decades, I've noticed that adoption facilitators have had a monopoly on the adoption discussion for generations and even formulated "Positive Adoption Language" (what they call PAL).

The PAL language disempowers those of us who have been told that we were orphaned as children yet astoundingly come from families—who are still alive and even searching and waiting for us! The PAL language[1] has prevented us from finding back what is rightfully ours early on in our lives. This book contains a condensed version of my evolutionary

---

*PAL contains words the industry wants us to use to normalize the adoption practice—but these words have stigmatized and reduced certain communities, parents, and children to a label, which has ultimately created and maintained the public's perception of adoption, and thus assisted with distorting the definition of family and manipulating international laws. Did you know these laws ignore our basic human rights?

journey into this discovery, depicted in excerpts taken from research and findings.

This collection of nine books offers a rare, yet universal look at the adoption practice from the inside out. I do not expect for anyone to believe anything I have discovered for myself. But, if you happen to read this, I hope you find some value in it. You might be interested in only one story, or many, and you don't need to read them in any particular order. I'm imperfect like all humans, and merely consider myself only to be someone led by curiosity. That's what fueled me the entire writing path. Along the way, I've also learned, shockingly, that we, "adoptees" receive poor treatment when we ask questions about our origin. Things need to change. These books might come in handy for the day you find yourself in need of defending your human rights position. I hope that, maybe, at least one story will validate one or two of your adoption experiences *because you matter*.

May you walk in awareness

Janine

Image: The city center of the adoptive community I
was sent to in the United States. Circa: 1970s

JOHNNY'S GROCERY STORE 1986

Introduction

Standing next to the cash registers, I'm a fourteen-year-old girl from Korea (dressed like Madonna and Michael Jackson), and I loiter in the magazine/book section of Johnny's grocery store. My hands are clutched to a random *True Story*, and I am totally engrossed in this journal spearheaded by a publisher who believes truth is stranger than fiction. The company began printing stories in 1919. By the 1950s, the magazine employed submitted stories from around the US involving young women reflecting on their lot in life. By the 1980s, the short stories I'm discovering are from real women who have somehow, someway gotten themselves into trouble: All I know is that I need to know more!

***

In front of me and my magazine of interest are other similar publications consisting of the hidden life of real people, like *True Love* and *True Confessions*. These short stories astound me. Do women go through such life events? It's unbelievable. I guess you could say I am sheltered and protected. You see, I'm a teen who attends a Presbyterian church at least twice a week. Thus far, I'm told certain women are "sinful" and blasphemous and should be burned at the stake (well, not that extreme, but at least kicked out of the church—if God knew what went on behind closed doors.) There's no internet in this day and age so everything is kept *private*. These were not stories from Hollywood stars. (Of course, according to my evangelical upbringing, we would expect Hollywood stars to live immoral lives.) No, these were secret narratives written by everyday women. I guess you could call them ordinary folk. And that is what made this magazine fantastic— profound really!

Pan out to a view of the grocery store from the sky: Johnny's is sandwiched between a tiny public laundromat and an old barbershop. The shot turns to the left: What comes to view? A decrepit middle school hidden by morning fog, a track and field of straw, and grass, and depression, 40 years after the 1940s depression. The town I was sent to has yet to be incorporated, and the land is somewhat being renewed somewhere under a layer of fallen oak leaves and nowhere. By now, the early 1980s, the internet, and the worldwide web have yet to go viral.

At this time, books and magazines are the closest thing I can get to a world outside of my own. I grab another magazine, run to the register, drop a dollar and whatever change, and race out to the street where a yellow bus of school kids pick me up for junior high.

Next scene: I'm sitting at a cafeteria lunch table engrossed in *True Confessions*. The lives of these women are insane! Fabulous! Next, I'm in the back of world history class (mind you—bored out of my freakin' mind). I'm sitting in the back, nose glued to someone's short story. It's not just one biography that intrigues me—it's every single one of them. Every life has captured me. Every story has enamored me.

I am simply at awe by the lives of those before us. *How the heck do women cope with disturbed parents, unapproved pregnancies, and disheveled relationships?* The way these women survive speed bumps, bruises, and barriers continue to astound me.

I go on with my own life. I graduate. I get married. I birth two daughters. I write out a memoir in an attempt to figure shit out. The next twenty years, pretty normal. Pretty routine. My girls graduate from high school. From college. They find decent jobs. I still love to read. My eyes are going out.

The recesses of my mind still fascinated by the lives of humans: We, humans, actually go through so much shit—shit we don't give ourselves credit for. In 2004, I learn about a community of people who have been (and still are) resisted and ousted from the mainstream. People who have been denied access to specific information that pertains to them, who have been abandoned again and again by a political system that claims it is protecting them. These are adopted people and the families left behind. Some adoptive parents might try to shield this community from you, I've learned, because of fear of reunion that comes from jealousy or misinformation. I've heard rumors of adoption agencies writing falsehoods on our documents to justify processing us.

I've been informed now on how certain pioneers armed with an agenda exploited communities and how we have (unknowingly-because they don't want us to know) been left out of the loop so that the profits can continue. Are you adopted or separated from a family member because of adoption? You need to be filled in. I want to fill you in on what I know cuz I believe you should know that you have rights.

Off the top of the iceberg ~ What I know is this:

#1) There are people who need our stories. These individuals are just hidden from our view. We need to put ourselves out there because maybe our stories will validate theirs.

#2) We should give ourselves the benefit of the doubt. We shouldn't shoot ourselves down before putting ourselves up there.

#3) It's easy to side with the top dogs (What's that saying? "It is easier for a camel to go through the eye of a needle than for a rich man to enter into the kingdom of heaven.")? But, we gain credit/karma points for siding with the poor. And just because some of us are poor, does not mean we are poor in spirit.

#4) Don't let authorities claim you're not qualified. If your soul wants to speak truth to power, you will feel curious. Your inner self will urge and pull you forth. That's your spirit talking. That's your human will, walking.

Why should we be receptive to the ups and downs of multiple adoption stories? When we allow the elite 1% to speak *for us*, they will share from their perspective, and naturally, this point of view is tainted with doing whatever is possible to protect their reputation. In other words, I've learned that what pro-adoption lobbyists claim to be "in the best interest of the child" is truly not always "in the best interest of the child."

Yes, we've given them the benefit of the doubt. But, isn't it time (for once in our lives) to give ourselves the benefit of the doubt?

If you're adopted, you have rights. We tend not to share our stories because we've been taught that whatever problems we encounter are our fault. We've been the scapegoats for the 1%. If we want to flip the script, then we must share our stories and listen to others outside the scope of what was traditionally "acceptable." (Remember, there's more of us than them.)

We have a right to write our own script even if it disagrees with those who planted us where we are. In fact, if we *do not* share our personal stories, they will eventually be forgotten or told by someone else. See, I believe our soul wants the life of us to be remembered by at least one, or two, maybe more. In order for people like us to obtain social equality, we need to fill the worldwide web with realistic adoption stories—stories that can convince the mainstream that we should have access to personal documents that pertain to us, birth certificates, and papers that reveal our true identities.

It is not uncommon for adoptive communities to disagree with the instinct to search (if we so choose).

The silver lining is not handed to us on a silver platter. We are responsible for finding for ourselves the shovel and digging the truth out for ourselves. We can contest all the reasons not to listen and not to know. But the truth will set future generations free--and it might even set ourselves free. If we want agencies to abide by the established laws based on human rights and social equality, we must be willing to voice the burdens we face. Otherwise, we allow for people with a profitable agenda to move us wherever they see fit and place us away from our roots, and all that comes with it: community, culture, and even our countries of birth—as if all of these are valueless.

Don't be afraid to speak out. Your human rights story could be the inspiration that opens the window to someone else's awakening. Let's draw open the curtains together.

THEY CALLED US ORPHANS

"You got passports?"

"Passports?" Dad asked and then confessed, "We didn't bring passports." This was just the Canadian border, and we're talkin' about the early 1970s.

A guard from the United States said, "Not yours." He concentrated on Dad's green eyes before he clarified, "I know you're American." The man in uniform pointed to my twin and me. We were toddlers at the time. "Where are their passports?"

"We didn't bring their passports." Dad was confused. "They're our daughters," He said of us.

In a monotone voice, the man at the Canadian and US Border said, "Pull off to the side. Get out. And stay by your vehicle." As if by routine, he waved a hand to a distant building, and Dad followed directions. Mom stayed with us and our two older brothers, while the uniformed man led Dad to the entrance of the building.

Once inside, he asked, "Where are they from?"

"You mean my daughters?" Dad said in disbelief. He never imagined that anyone would question our status as his daughters. "Korea" was his answer.

"If they don't have passports, I could send them back," the man said.

"No, no, no. They're American," Dad emphasized. We were what our parents referred to as a first-rate family. "My daughters don't even speak Korean. We got them when they were babies."

Dad didn't think to bring our adoption papers on this vacation. He had no idea that by this time, they could accuse him of harboring illegal aliens. Adoption agencies didn't require applicants to seek US citizenship for the children they wanted to adopt. That would have slowed down the process, and fewer people would apply.

"They've been adopted," Dad explained, "Holt adopted them from Korea, and we adopted them from Holt. We got them when they were babies."

See, the adoption pioneers needed for adoption to be treated as normal as giving birth, and our parents tried their best. For years, we all tried our best. And we did good. In fact, I think we did a fantastic job. We played the part magnificently. And we still have great affection for each other.

At last, my dad was able to convince the guard that there was no foul play.

Once back into the camper and over the border, Dad told Mom the details of what had happened inside the building. Later, he jotted a note in a journal to mark the date of the hair-raising episode: "This is my last trip to Canada."

Of course, my twin and I were much too young to be told about the potential fiasco, and once we got old enough to maybe comprehend the potential magnitude, well, the incident was long forgotten. Since my twin and I were never told, we also didn't know, and because we didn't know, we never thought to apply for our US citizenship. We were walking around stateless for twenty-five years! My twin and I wouldn't find out that we were not US citizens until after Mom died. In fact, I remember seeing our Green Cards for the first time, and in awe that we were literally called Aliens. By this time, decades after our adoption—Illegal Aliens.

~Don Ho

It's better for the adoption profiteers if we, adoptees, don't know that we came from a family because if we don't know, we won't investigate. If we let bygones be bygones and trust their evangelical judgment as if it is worth more than ours (as if we shouldn't know), and if we give them the benefit of the doubt, the industry grows. And it has. When it's lucrative for the agencies, they determine what's right and wrong, and everything stays the same. Stagnant. No growth. No evolution. No revolution. They determine the laws. We nod and smile along.

If we remain positive and accept what is, if we tend to pay attention to the beauty of the practice but not examine the insides, we will be less likely to give ourselves the benefit of the doubt, and we will forgo the potential beauty of our birth culture, and if we forgo the potential of our birth culture, it's harder to see the beauty within ourselves.

There comes a point in time when we must acknowledge that we are more than our nationality, and we are bigger than our ethnicity. There comes a time when we have an aha moment. What is that aha moment? It's sort of like a revelation. A revelation is when we put all the pieces together to see the bigger picture. When we see the bigger picture, we can see ourselves through the realm of reality and truth. The truth is we belong to a blood family that is connected to a tribal community, and this community is big and bright and bold with life, and we should be proud of the ties to blood that each of us has. We should not play small and reduce our human nature—for we are all connected. We belong to something bigger and more expansive. We belong to life itself. Always remember that you are more than an American (as wonderfully dramatic as that can be). Together, we make up the collective of great. ...And this is good.

***

Excerpt from
"Tiny Bubbles"
AMERICANIZED '72
A Generation-X Coming-of-Age
(& Identity) Adoption Story

THEY CALLED US LUCKY

"So, Dad, Umm. Uh, what do you think about Jenette and me going to Korea?" I ask without thinking one day in 2004.

Dad smiles. "I think it's great. Did you know I took two hundred trips for Boeing?" He staggers along the neighborhood cul-de-sac, pushing a Rollator—an updated dark-blue four-wheeled walker for balance. Dad's hair has turned completely white, emphasizing intense green eyes. As he grasps the handles for balance, he slouches so that even though I'm only five feet tall, we're practically at eye level. Our journey together has been long. When I was growing up in the 1970s to early eighties, Dad was a perfect swan. He was a Christian teacher, elder, youth group leader, choir director, and Boy Scout leader for a small community church. He preached the moral values of yesterday, where followers lived toward a vision of success and problems got solved in a day's episode. You can't get any more glorious than that.

That is until Dad reached the age of fifty-four when he began to hang glide. On October 20, 1984, he unintentionally "flew the coop." His life changed for the worse—or for the better—depending on how one chooses to look at it. On his seventh high-altitude flight, the glider folded during mid-flight, causing him to fall 100 feet through a tree, hitting his head several times on the branches. Thus began his life as a "disabled" person. He was forced to retire early from his engineering job, where he was employed for thirty-two years. Due to his newly inflicted disability, his schedule was reduced to mainly reading and watching television while confined to a recliner. His motto went from, "Don't just sit there. Do something" to "Don't just do something. Sit there."

From the age of twelve, my twin and I have been emotionally supporting Dad throughout his recovery, providing care as he learned to adapt and accept his new physical limitations. We figure that if our family can overcome such a large life bump, we can pretty much overcome anything. Although Dad isn't entirely independent after his injury, his mind and heart are in sync, and he listens to issues of mine without brawls or snarls.

"Umm. Uh, Dad? Uh, what do you think . . . ." Trudging beside him on the South Seattle cement, I study him, not knowing how to ask the question without putting it bluntly. "What do you think about Jenette and me finding our birth parents?" It's a topic we've never discussed.

"What?"

"What do you think," I ask, now shouting, "about us finding our birth parents?"

His smile collapses, and he jerks and jiggles the Rollator to a stop, almost losing his balance. "I don't like it."

I'm surprised by his quick response. "Why?" I ask. By this time in our lives, I thought my sister and I had demonstrated our loyalties to him, and so, I hoped, he wouldn't think we were going to abandon him.

He's silent for a moment and then shakes his head. "I just don't."

"Can you give me a reason?"

"I don't like it." He rolls again. "I'm your father."

"Yeah. I can understand your feelings. I mean... I know I wouldn't be able to talk to Mom about this if she was still alive. But I always thought you were so much more open-minded."

"You're right, Janine." Dad's light ivory face stiffens, and forehead creases appear. "She wouldn't like it either."

"There's no way I could look for my birth parents if Mom was still around," I stutter, suddenly feeling childish. "Or, at least, I'd have to keep it a secret. And I would feel guilty too. But now it's the Gathering in Seoul. Adoptees from around the world are coming together for the 50-year reunion of overseas adoption. Our birth parents might be looking for us."

Dad lurches to another gallant stop. "I'm your father," he says, then starts rolling again.

I watch him push the Rollator around—each step choppy. He's seventy-three, but I've been told he could pass in age from anywhere between sixty to eighty years old. I think it's because of his injury.

Long ago, before Dad's injury, he was robust and forthright. He's probably the only person I know of who had the audacity to chase a state cop down a street for close to a mile because the officer pulled out in front of my parents and, as Dad tells the story with a laugh, "forced me to skid and veer to the next lane. The cop was totally in the wrong! He almost caused an accident, and it would have been his fault! If I had a ticket book, I'd slap him with a ticket!" This type of righteousness, blended with a hearty sense of humor over the cop's immediate apology, is the kind of person Dad used to be. If someone did something wrong—according to the rules belonging to the "Top Swan," Dad was determined to call the individual on his mistake and make him pay. My parents were good old-fashioned right-winged swans intent on flying the "right" way! The type of folks who fluffed their feathers at a Billy Graham revival meeting and crooned bestowing all power to the "Great Big Bird," then went home and pecked at their ugly ducklings for veering off course during the hour-long lecture while at the same time calling us *lucky*.

The afternoon breeze rustles Dad's loose-fitting red T-shirt and Navy sweatpants as he circles the cul-de-sac at a snail's pace. Going around and around seems to reflect our lives together. Life appears to have always revolved around him. It's not easy to fly away when I see that's he's been grounded for the most part. Our family now laughs a lot. I enjoy being there for him, just as he's been around for me.

Dad's statement echoes in my mind, *I'm your father.*

I nod and nudge his elbow. "You'll always be my Dad. No matter what. But don't you think? Don't you think that the Korean population? When they hear what a great father you've been. How open-minded you are. Don't you think they'll find honor in that? Don't you think you'll get respect for that?"

Dad digests my words as he continues to push his Rollator along the sidewalk. Giant houses in the latest Pacific Northwest colors of rust, cocoa, evergreen, and sunflower gaze down at us. Wobbling ahead, he focuses on a bumper sticker on the wheeled walker. It was a Father's Day gift Jenette bought at the Boeing Museum of Flight that reads: "I'd rather be flying." For thirty-two years, he had been employed as a Boeing mechanical engineer, working on satellites, airplanes, the secretive "black box," and other projects he's kept private. After his injury, that part of his life came to a shocking halt, prompting twenty years of searching for the way out of suffering, which led to a move beyond Christianity and an expansion of awareness that includes world religions and spirituality.

"Don't you think our birth parents will be grateful? And who knows?" I shrug. "Maybe we can even take you to Korea so you can meet them."

"Oh, no." Dad grimaces. "I don't want to go to Korea. I should stay in America. Nothing beats the United States."

My parents have always been proud to be Americans and with that came the impression that South Korea was a horrible country—a place that would have treated Jenette and me with disdain. Korea is a place where we would have either starved to death or become prostitutes. No one even needed to say this verbally—although the implication has been made. It was felt in the air by our parents' unintentional arrogance. Their disregard for other flocks, when we were kids, implied that we should deny our heritage and never consider making a voyage to such foreign soil. It's been my curiosity that makes the trip more appealing rather than appalling like Dad sees it.

If I were any younger, I wouldn't go; just the thought might have seriously jeopardized my relationship with my parents. To think that I belong to another flock—a Korean family—would have caused my adoptive parents to feel bad, risking potential pain for everyone involved. I can't even imagine bringing up the topic of other parents around my late adoptive mother. Our relationship as a "real" mother and daughter could have been questioned. Nope. Out of respect for my adoptive mother, I wouldn't take the risk if she was still alive. Doing a search would be a serious violation, and dishonor for all Mom did for us. I would hate to jeopardize our relationship by following up on my own curiosity.

I nudge Dad's arm a little disappointed that he is so afraid of what I'll find. It's not my intention to replace him if that's what he thinks. "Don't you think Mom understands now?" Trying to make him feel better. "She's probably watching us from heaven. I'm sure she's cheering for us."

"What?" My dad hollers without realizing our neighbors can probably hear our conversation.

"Mom understands now," I say discreetly.

"What?" Dad blares.

20

"Now that Mom is in heaven, she sees us from a more loving perspective. She understands!" Embarrassed, I scan the neighborhood, hoping no one is listening.

Dad nods but doesn't say anything, and we continue to walk in large cul de sac circles. I assure myself that going will be the right thing. My husband had told me that he plans to take care of Dad, the kids (including Jenette's two), the house, and the dog. "I think it's time," he had said even though he worried for me. "You should go. Don't worry. I've got everything under control." He had also encouraged me years back to become a U.S. citizen when I found out upon Mom's death that my parents never applied for Jenette and my citizenship—it wasn't required upon adopting us. According to documents, we were still "alien immigrants" and foreign children—floaters between two nations. Throughout my twenties, I had been more loyal to Dad than to myself. Now, in my early thirties with my own family, it might be time to consider my own past, at last.

As I round another circle with Dad, I promise myself that I will definitely make the trip with Jenette even though he is a bit unsettled at the thought. I enter the house through the garage door, while he turns away from me to open the side gate, a route with fewer bumps and barriers. Upon taking our separate routes to get inside, Dad shouts one of his most popular words of wisdom, "One thing is for sure, Janine. Change is the only constant in life."

***

Excerpt from
"Change is a Constant"
THE SEARCH FOR MOTHER MISSING
A Peek Inside International Adoption

THEY CALLED US ALIENS

My American name is Monte Haines, and my Korean name is Han Ho Kyu. At age eight, I arrived in Iowa almost 6500 miles from Seoul, South Korea. Long golden cornfields, woodlands of elm, and hickory covered this earthly terrain. Basement ramblers strewn about vacant neighborhoods fronted by freshly mowed lawns thanks to John Deere tractors, replacing South Korea's city cemented streets—streets I had been used to roaming. I felt like I was left stranded in the middle of a foreign land. I was scared and had no idea where I was.

From the agency, employees sent me to my first adoptive family: Mr. and Mrs. Hormmans, a white couple with two older boys. The whole family had various colors of hair, just like the land's earthy terrain. One of my first memories is the way everyone stared at me when I arrived. They just kept looking at me strangely.

I was given a small room to sleep in, and all went pretty well for the next couple of months, despite the language barrier. Then it started: the physical, mental, and sexual abuses. This went on for about six months to a year. My adoptive father used to hit me if I didn't do what he wanted. I attended school with black and blue bruises on my arms and my back. If anyone asked what had happened, I claimed I had fallen down the stairs to protect my adoptive father from getting into trouble.

Sometimes my adoptive father locked me in the closet without food and water. They left me there all day—sometimes for many days. On some bone-chilly Iowan winter days, they made me undress and sent me outside completely naked, tied my hands and feet to two trees, and hollered for their two black Doberman Pinschers to nip at my legs as punishment or they shouted for the dogs to chase me around the house. When I came home late from school one day, my dad yanked my right foot and broke one of my toes as punishment. This abuse persisted until a teacher called the Child Protection Agency to investigate the family. Authorities removed me from my adoptive parents' home and sent me to foster care.

I stayed in five different foster homes. The living quarters were crowded, and I mostly slept on the floor. I felt like tossed around garbage—like they didn't want me at all. I hid in inconspicuous spaces and remained out of sight for as long as I could. Eventually, the social workers found a family who wanted to adopt me, but they weren't allowed because they had too many kids, including a son named Monte. I did stay at the house for a while, but I was eventually sent to another foster family.

July of 1981, Holt International Children Services sent me to Mr. and Mrs. Haines. At the age of eleven, I stood in front of a judge and was legally adopted by them. I gained an adoptive brother named John, who was five years older than I, and like a real brother, we did everything together. We formed a real friendship. I assumed that this family would be good for me. I finally found a family who wanted me, and I was happy.

My assumption of the happily-ever-after adoption disappeared when I attended school. The students called me names and made fun of me. I ran out of the building and found a place to hide. While crying, I thought, what did I do wrong? Why am I so different from the other kids?

During the summer, my nightmare came back to haunt me. Mr. Haines, my new adopted father, a man with a good reputation within the community, abused me physically, mentally, and sexually. After coming home from playing outside, my dad hit me with a breadboard so hard that I blacked out. Other times my dad crept into my room at night and crawled into bed with me. I endured this for a long time. He also abused my older, adopted brother.

My dad kicked my brother out of the house when he was sixteen-years-old, and I didn't get to see him for a very long time. I was only eleven at the time and now the only child left in the household. As a consequence, all the abuse was then focused on me. My mom was too scared to leave or to call the cops. If I didn't mow the lawn, rake the grass, and other chores correctly, my adoptive father would slam my head against a concrete wall. This seemed to go on all the time. My mom couldn't handle the abuse and finally divorced him.

My adoptive father moved himself and me to Colorado, along with a friend of mine and his mom, who moved in with us. It seemed like the living conditions were going well until one day, a police officer pulled me from class and told me that my dad was arrested for child abuse against my friend and me. My friend's mom called the cops.

I had to leave Colorado to live with my adoptive mom. I didn't get along with her very well due to being previously abandoned by her, but she treated me better than my father did. I ran away from home and headed for the airport, trying to go back home to Korea, where I belonged.

After I had graduated from high school, I enlisted in the United States Army. Because the military enlistment did not require proof of US citizenship, I never doubted my status as a US citizen. I served in the Gulf War for three and a half years and lost many friends there. When I returned to civilian life, it was hard for me to sleep at night. I woke from nightmares, and I couldn't forget the images of war. Some people call this Gulf War Syndrome or Post Traumatic Stress Disorder.

After the military, I found a job as a truck driver. On February 27, 2001, my driving partner and I were assigned to take a load to the East Coast. When I came to the checkpoint, the authorities were waiting for us. My driving partner didn't tell me he had planted drugs in the truck's trailer.

I spent my time in a jail cell where I was locked up full-time, in prison, and also in an immigration holding detention center. Inside, there seemed to be around thirty Korean adoptees at the risk of being deported. I learned later that every state has these detention centers. In each one of these, you'll find ten to twenty Korean adoptees, standing by to be deported back to Korea.

My older brother, John, and I fought my case to the best of our ability and to the point of exhaustion from explaining my defense. Eventually, I gave up hope and told him to stop helping me. I knew it was a lost cause.

On December 25th, 2005, I was released on house arrest and required to report monthly to the US Immigration and Customs Enforcement (ICE), a Department of Homeland Security. I was required to go to Houston, Texas, where the Korean consul was located to obtain a passport. There, I was not allowed to leave the state. I was told my name was not recorded in their computer.

"What?!" I was shocked. "Why not?"

"Your situation is kind of strange to us," the man from the Immigration Office told me.

I asked again, "Why?"

"You're adopted, but you're not a US citizen," he said.

Completely shocked, I was like, "I am a US citizen. I was adopted in '81. The law says if you're adopted by an American citizen, you are an American US citizen." During my visit, I asked, "Why can't you help me?"

His only response was that he was afraid of Homeland Security.

I went back to my American home empty-handed and lived out of my car. Fortunately, I found a job with a construction company and regularly reported to the ICE office while applying for a passport to Korea.

On August 20, 2008, my older brother, John, killed himself with a shotgun. The trauma for me was unbearable, and I didn't report to ICE that month as required. When an immigration officer called me, I simply stated, "I didn't report because my brother died."

Only two months later, officers in full SWAT uniforms barged into my room—a garage turned into a living space—pointing handguns and M16 assault rifles at me while shouting, "Get on the ground!" as if I had been a convicted terrorist. They pushed my knees onto the floor, handcuffed my wrists together, and ushered me back to a detention center. I was accused of threatening a deportation officer, but they didn't believe me when I told them this was not true. Instead, I was thrown back into a cell, with the door locked behind me.

When I stood in front of the Immigration Judge, he scolded: "You are not allowed in *my* country. This is *my* country. This is *my* land. I want you out of it."

On November 4, 2009, I was deported back to Korea, wearing only jeans and a T-shirt. I had only twenty dollars on me, I couldn't speak the language, and I didn't know where to go. All forms of my identification and personal documents were confiscated. My escorts, four men and one woman dressed in civilian clothes, basically dropped me off at the Incheon Airport and left me there on the gray tarmac more than six thousand miles away from everything I knew for almost forty years. Forever gone were the strewn-about basement ramblers, long golden cornfields, woodlands of elm, and hickory. Rather, South Korea's city cemented streets—streets I would roam as a homeless person—replaced the John Deere tractor-mowed lawns. Grey low winter clouds chilled me to the bone. Again, I felt stranded in a foreign land. No longer able to speak the Korean language, I was scared and had no idea where to go.

Excerpt from
"Deported"
THE "UNKNOWN" CULTURE CLUB
Korean Adoptees, Then and Now
*As remembered by Monte Haines, aka Han Ho Kyu, still living in Korea today.

THEY CALLED US ANTI-ADOPTION

I WAS BORN IN Haiti in 1979 and adopted in 1984 by a single French woman. The story of my abandonment then boiled down to a few vague lines and other falsehoods written in my adoption file. It wasn't until 2002 that I managed to find my Haitian family and only then that I learned the truth about my adoption.

There are three entities in me:
   *Manassé, this Haitian child who arrived in France in 1984
   *Christophe, the perfect little French boy who started to exist in 1984
   *Tinan, who appeared in 2004
It is not easy for three people to inhabit the same body.

Excerpt 1
My Haitian mother, Iliasia, could not have children (despite numerous attempts) and her sterility

made her very unhappy. One day, Iliasia's husband proposed that he leave Haiti for the United States (prompted by his growing prosperity) and Iliasia accepted the idea. After they sold all of their possessions, her husband actually left for the United States leaving Illiasia homeless, penniless, and alone with her infertility. After several years of misery, Iliasia met another Haitian man and their union produced a daughter who died five days after birth. Iliasia despaired after the infant's death. But one day, my older brother was born, a frail child who was often ill when he was young. He survived but, at the same time, our parent's relationship began to deteriorate.

Things got worse after the arrival of their second child. My mother, 38-years-old at the time of my birth, baptized me as Manassé. Like my brother, I was also fragile and needed care. During my early childhood, Iliasia found herself, once again, without a partner and without work. This time, however, she carried two young children in her arms. Our survival became precarious. In Haiti at the time, it was customary to entrust children, for short periods of time, in a type of boarding school run by a religious congregation that received foreign aid. Children placed in their care temporarily always belonged to their Haitian parents. The nursery was built to give children in need some help such as food, medicine, and education. My big brother was placed in a facility of this type not far from our hometown, but he failed to adapt. Iliasia brought him packages, but the gifts were turned away, and the children remained poor as a result.

Iliasia retrieved my older brother, who was then in very poor health, even though she was still unable to provide for her two sons. She decided to put me in the home of Miss Marthe in Gros Morne, seventy-five miles away, which was a nursery of about forty children. It operated on a principle of exchange with France. A man, named Wisly, placed Haitian children with French host families so that they could get treatment and receive an education. He then brought them back to Haiti in either a few months or a few years.

It was expected that a permanent relationship would be maintained between the adoptive French family and the Haitian one, except that the children who were adopted to France never returned to Haiti! Haitian parents had very little information about their children, or about their French guardians, and contact was cut off after only a few months. Wisly, who was supposed to serve as a bridge between the two countries and the two families, vanished. Rumors also circulated that children had died or had been used for organ trafficking. From all of those who went missing at the time, only the two oldest children from the nursery managed to return to Haiti as adults to find their families. I was the third to take advantage of this opportunity but, among the three children who returned, no one has been able to find information about the other missing children.

I met with Haitian mothers of adoption loss, the victims of child trafficking still left behind. They shared both their pain, but also their hope, with me. I promised to look for their roughly forty missing sons and daughters once I was back in France. This recovery mission has become my raison d'être.

Between 2002 and 2003, I returned to Haiti. I took up the responsibility of financing the education of my newly-discovered little brother and sister. I felt compelled to take on the burden for my family and for all to go well yet, despite our regular exchanges, I felt more and more foreign and alienated from my homeland.

Excerpt 2

In 2002, I believed that I was at a crossroads in my life, but I am now starting to realize that that was not the case. In 2003, I felt great doubt. On my first trip to Haiti, I thought that I belonged to two worlds. It occurs to me now that I do not belong to either. When I left France, I needed to find my roots because I did not feel at home there. But, as the years go by, I realize I am no more at home in Haiti. I have friends and a lot of people who appreciate and support me but, yet, I feel alone and out of context. I wander in a no-man's land, ill-defined, trying to build upon my shaky foundation, while it continually gives way under my feet. Sometimes, I struggle to keep my balance and not to get lost in the grey area of adoption. Sometimes, I lose my grip completely and falter. I do not have vertigo, but every time I stumble, my heart drops, and I feel worse. I sometimes struggle with madness. To keep my feet firmly planted on the ground, I have to focus my effort on concrete and logical things to keep sane. In high school, and at the beginning of my graduate studies, I was not very good in math (despite my appetite for science). I improved significantly, however, as my need for roots intensified, I would seek concrete, immutable certainties, as well as rigor and logic in order to stay grounded.

My adoptive mother does not understand me. Our relationship is riddled with disputes and conflict. I have no adoptive father, someone to balance her authority. I also feel that my girlfriend does not fully understand me, which has caused issues between us, as she moves so easily in the world as she pursues her dreams. Despite my best efforts, I cannot get closer to her. My Haitian family does not understand me, either. My older Haitian brother is the only one with whom I have a healthy and peaceful relationship with, but we communicate infrequently via e-mail and sometimes on the phone. I don't blame anyone. There is no need to do math to realize that I am the common denominator in all of these relationships.

In 2004, tensions with my Haitian family were high and conflicts with my adoptive mother were so destructive that I decided to finally cut ties with my French family in order to survive.

Excerpt 3

Locked in an icy cocoon, my older brother sends me e-mail that I do not read because I'm barricaded in my solitude. My fiancée no longer talks to me. I'm gone. It is the last heartbeat of Christophe (my French name). Someone (or some thing) else is still present, but the little French boy who was much loved by his adoptive mother, has died.

Failing to mourn for myself, I try to remove all traces of who I was. I separate from my girlfriend, I move, change my phone number, and register with the liste rouge. I left without warning anyone — not even my friends. I leave fake addresses so that my adoptive mother cannot find me. I threw out all objects that remind me of my past life.

I am no longer Christophe. To continue to exist, I become Tinan. More than a name, it is a concept, a means of survival, an identity that I have to build piece-by-piece. I untangle who I was supposed to be, to erase my reflexes, my ingrained habits. I reset my brain like a hard drive to be wired before installing a new operating system. Thus, I continue to live my own way. I do my best to move forward, despite the obstacles. I help others whenever I am able, those who firmly believe that life is beautiful. I fulfill my duties, I try to accomplish my mission, to provide as much happiness as possible. It's all that I can do to keep from giving up.

I model Tinan like a cyborg. My body is what it is, but my brain can do whatever it wants. To get rid of anything that resembles a genetic disorder, I choose to become impervious to certain sensations like pain, hunger, thirst, fatigue, stress, cold, or anxiety. I used to get sick very often, but I won't get sick anymore. I used to be very ticklish, now that is over. I decided that I will no longer feel anger and that I will never cry again. The ataraxia is not far.

What is Tinan's future? I know I cannot keep my life in a robotic state but, for now, I haven't found another solution. Gradually, my shell became a prison that I could not escape with bars forged by my sensitivity, my weakness, my fears, my shyness, my lack of confidence, and my need for love.

The years pass and I am hyperactive. I teach salsa. I create a dance company. I invent choreographies. I play the saxophone in several bands. I study music very intensely, including its composition and its history. I write and arrange different styles for multiple groups and I feel a great need to create and to make art. I know that soon I will resign from the Department of Education. As a physics teacher, I am cast in a role that is not creative enough. My days are too long and my nights are too short. My body is worn, but numb, I do not listen to its warnings. I used to take up to ten micro-naps several times a day, which allowed me to recover partly from my lack of rest. I've become efficient in the art of analysis, making syntheses, and creating models to understand how things work. These new capabilities are very helpful to me when I teach, allowing me to better understand the difficulties of my students and to better deconstruct the steps involved with reasoning or the individual components of various movements so that I can explain it in detail, make it easy to grasp, and accessible to anyone.

Excerpt 4

I am a free and lonely man, but I cannot find stability, because it would require that I accept the brute part of my being, which I refuse. I try hard to contain the demon which is imprisoned in my cell, but it is a constant struggle against myself. I'm finally starting to understand the exact nature of this monstrous creature. It is the small child within me, Manassé, whose growth and life are suddenly arrested at the age of four and-a-half, when he fell into this nightmare without end, sent far from his family, from his country, far from the love of his Haitian mother.

By dint of incarceration, secretly declining the hostile world that was offered to him as a gift, Manassé eventually became a wild beast, extremely violent, and dangerous (but with a pure soul of a fragile child). What a paradox! The being I consigned to oblivion in 2004 was Christophe. Yet Manassé was there for twenty years. If I want to live in peace, I have to release the prisoner. But the wrath of Manassé is so big that it will destroy everything in its path, devouring Tinan (as it did Christophe). What will become of me if I open Manassé's cage? Will I be a monster? My integrated personality and these twenty long years of frustration and pent-up anger will lead me to the irreparable. As a result, I cannot love myself or accept love from anybody. To calm Manassé's anger, I would have to admit that what happened to me was not my fault. I should also forgive the adults responsible, even if they are guilty.

I hold enormous grudges against my two mothers.

In 1984, Iliasia did not abandon me. She dropped me off at a boarding school for a few months in the hopes of getting me back to full health. She was deceived into signing an "abandonment for adoption" paper. Like the majority of Haitian mothers at the time, she could not read. It made no difference to Manassé whether or not Iliasia had abandoned him voluntarily the day he was forced to board a plane for nowhere without understanding what was happening. It was her responsibility to look after her son and to not be manipulated. Ignorance might have been a mitigating factor, but it was, by no means, an excuse.

My adoptive mother has always believed that I should thank her for "saving" me. How can you thank someone for removing you from family roots? How can we pretend that money and a Parisian apartment are worth more than a Haitian mother's love? This is absurd, of course! Adoption, itself, is an absurd idea. It should be a workaround, a last resort, the ultimate solution before euthanasia. Instead, it has become the answer to the whims and desires of Western families. They adopt for themselves because they cannot have children, because they need someone to inherit their hopes and frustrations, or because they want to brag that they've saved a little dark-skinned child from certain death. I was adopted by a French woman for these three reasons and, for these three reasons, I can never forgive her.

***

Before learning the truth about his adoption, Tinan Leroy thought (as most French people do), that it was a good thing. He even felt guilty for not being grateful to his adoptive mother. But a return to his home country of Haiti, the subsequent years spent searching, investigating, studying, and meeting a lot of other adoptees, and writing the book,

Magnitude 7.3, led him to this horrible conclusion: Inter-country adoption is just a huge marketplace where children are sold, resold, exchanged, and trafficked without any real regard for their actual welfare. Many adoptions have dramatic endings, but these numerous cases are rarely reported. The truth is that adopted children are nothing more than luxury goods! The powerful adoption lobby prohibits any study showing this aspect of the industry, which is the reason Tinan is firmly determined to reveal the hidden face of adoption in order to seek some redress for the victims of this particular type of trafficking.

***

Excerpt from
"Magnitude 7.3"
ADOPTIONLAND
From Orphans to Activists

Update: On October 19, 2014, Tinan Leroy passed away from heart failure. While he was alive, Tinan asked that fellow adoptees support his story "because the French will not acknowledge the hidden side of international adoption." The love affair with the practice of adoption has become a global crisis. During Tinan's short life, he was a very talented man: an author, a physics professor, a saxophone player, and a choreographer, but he confided that he felt alone. His friends believe that his adopter deleted his Facebook, YouTube, author, and memorial pages. A lack of support from adopters is reported as a common problem for adopted people who search for their families. Our hope is to keep Tinan's memory alive through this book. Tinan wanted this book to reach the mainstream public. Please consider donating copies on his behalf to educational institutions and organizations.

THEY CALLED US ANGRY

"As we call out your number," Sister Ursula said, "please step forward to claim your child. Examine the child we selected for you. If it's satisfactory, take it to your home and treat it as you would your own flesh and blood."
~From Mail Order Kid by Marilyn Coffer pg. 19

***

The American children loaded onto trains as early as 1854 were not necessarily unwanted, despite some historical accounts that refer to them as waifs or foundlings, but came from families. The children were led to believe that they were orphaned and labeled as such on documents (which then denied them access to birth certificates and other related documents which might have helped them locate, identify, and reunite with their relatives years later). Just one example of this is a woman by the name of Teresa Martin, who, at age 73, returned to the hospital where she was born in 1906. The nuns turned her away with a terse response: "Your case is closed."

In the PBS documentary, Orphan Trains, produced and directed by Janet Graham and Edward Gray, readings from the writings and letters of now-deceased children can be heard transforming stories from the past into vivid narratives. Personal accounts reveal the fear, turmoil, and loss they experienced as children making the forced trek from New York City into unknown areas out West.

Lorraine Williams remembered the details (even though she was only four at the time): "The big day came, and we arrived on a Sunday in Kirksville, Missouri, at the Presbyterian church. We marched down the aisle, thirteen of us, and they would walk past us, and you were viewed. And that's a strange feeling. You'd never been looked at in that way before. You'd never seen people looking all around you."

Elliott Hoffman Bobo, age eight, felt insecure at the public viewings and articulated what many others sensed: "I wasn't very comfortable up on that stage because I didn't know where I was going to go. And I was old enough to realize that there could be a lot of mistakes."

Lee Nailing, also eight, mentioned how he intentionally placed a pink envelope given to him by his father into his coat pocket that contained his address. His father told him to be sure to let him know when he and his brothers got to their destination. The next morning, Lee immediately reached into his pocket, but the envelope was gone. "I was kind of heartbroken, of course." He asked for help, but "one of the caretakers came by and asked us what we were doing and [we] told her that we were looking for the envelope. I was afraid to tell her anything else because punishment sometimes was a little severe. And she told me to get up, get in my seat, [because] where I was going I would not need that envelope."

By the time Lee reached a small town in Texas, he had reported that there were about twenty-five children left, including his two-year-old brother. He watched as a couple took him away. "There again, I -- I felt terrible because I knew I was losing a brother right there. And they took Gerald over to the table, did the paperwork, and he was just happy as he could be until they started out the door, and he suddenly realized that he was losing his brothers. And he turned around and screamed right loud for his 'bruvvers.' And, of course, that broke my heart again."

Someone chose Lee and, as a consequence, "After two or three years, going back to New York was just past thinking." Lee eventually became acclimated to his situation and even reported being happy. However, he said, "My adoptive mother, Mrs. Nailling, she lived with a horror that I would eventually go back to New York to my biological people." He further explained, "I don't imagine I would have gone back if I'd have had the chance, but even after I was grown, she had that horror."

Regarding the arrival into her new loving family, Claretta Miller, age nine, said, "I knew that this was going to be my home from then on, but it seemed like it just kind of hit me when I got here that I had left everything behind, which I had. I didn't have my sister anymore. I didn't have my parents anymore. I didn't have any friends. They were total strangers. It just caught up with me all at once. But [the woman who chose her] was with me, Mrs. Carmen. She never left me for a minute. And she helped me get into bed, and that's when I began to cry. [...] was when the emotion hit me, I think, when I went to get into bed. I still felt all alone, and yet I knew there was someone around me, but they were strangers. I didn't know them from Adam."

Like many children from similarly-large migrations even today, Alice Ayler was aware of her lower status in relation to the other children in her new adoptive surroundings, "Bad blood. That's what they used to consider it. We kids from New York were of inferior stock."

However, she spoke of being able to become a good mother because of the westward move: "I got to do what I was capable of doing, making something of myself, being a good mother." Of her traumatic beginnings, she said, "It hurt awfully bad, being separated from my family."

Justifying the practice, and affirming that it needs to continue, are common refrains from those who have been adopted. It is something a great many feel obligated to do, becoming almost a habit meant to gain approval after sharing their not-so-positive experiences. A happy ending tends to leave the impression that all is well that ends well. Yet, the happy ending had more to do with the adopted person's own will and tenacity to survive, despite being adopted, rather than to the adoption itself.

Marilyn June Coffey, author of Mail-Order Kid: An Orphan Train Rider's Story, gave a detailed depiction of the entire landscape during that time, as well as an account of a four-year-old girl sent to

Kansas from New York. Coffey mentions that fifty or so orphan-train riders shed tears as they described their childhoods during a reunion decades later.

A rivalry for children erupted between the Protestant and Catholic denominations (from a competing orphanage started by Sister Irene versus the founder of Children's Aid Society (CAS), Charles Loring Brace). When it came to placing children for adoption, religious affiliation was a significant factor: "Brace's Protestant Group, The CAS, soon made Catholic enemies." Coffey briefly hinted at an internal competition between Brace and the Catholic co-founders of Foundlings Hospital. "They [Catholic sisters] hated the way Brace 'snatched' children off the streets and sent them out of the city. They accused him of putting Catholic children into Protestant homes in order to convert them." Furthermore, "because of the jealousy," the staff at New York Foundling Hospital sent Jewish and Protestant babies and toddlers out to the rural Catholic homes. The nuns copied some of Brace's techniques to assist with what was at first called "Baby Trains," then later referred to as "Mercy Trains" by relying on local priests to send about 30,000 children out into the fields.

Coffey mentioned that the orphan train riders suffered "Physical, intellectual, and emotional wounds" and "....a displacement much like an 'exhaustion from a prolonged trauma.'" Some children relayed tales of being treated well or petted and pampered (in the author's words), while others were subjected to abuse. Whether they were foster or adoptive guardians, most of the adult strangers involved were not motivated to treat the children well (because they believed that they were already doing the children a favor by allowing them into their homes in the first place).

A number of the children even needed to learn a new language when they were moved across the country, as was the case with Teresa Martin, the protagonist of Mail-Order Kid, a child presented as an orphan and sent to Hays, Kansas, by the Catholic sisters. Hays was a "rough and tough town in its early years of 1867, at one time sporting 37 liquor establishments." A group of Russian Volga Germans (initially named after the longest river in Russia) initially settled in the area to farm.

Little Teresa, whose mother was Jewish, did not know where she was going until she reached her destination. Once there, ministers announced the news to the waiting couples and farmers: "'As we call out your number,' Sister Ursula said, 'Please step forward to claim your child. Examine the child we selected for you. If it's satisfactory, take it to your home and treat it as you would your own flesh and blood.'"

Teresa was one of those children. An elderly German couple with grown children took her by the hand, but they were interrupted by other interested adults:

"Pardon me [...] I'm wondering if I could buy this little girl from you?"

"You wish to buy this child?" the nun asked, but rejected the request because the man was Presbyterian and not Catholic. "I'm afraid it's out of the question. If you were Catholic, we would perhaps consider it."

Teresa remembered the Presbyterian couple offering to take her for cash, but the Catholic man refused to accept because of his Protestant affiliation. The Catholic mother Teresa had been assigned to even arrogantly "switched her long skirt away" and hissed "Jude" as they walked away with Teresa in tow, who did not understand the insult.

At such a young age, Teresa watched these exchanges while the adults selected the other children. She trembled while thinking, "I won't see my mother and father, but strangers pretending to be my parents. Why are the Sisters doing this?"

Adoptive Home

Once arriving at the isolated house on the outskirts of Schoenchen (founded in 1877 and known as the German Capital of Kansas), Teresa was made to sit on the lap of her new father while he drank a beer (as if she were already his child). Her new mother slapped her face that first night before bed because the four-year-old girl had not yet learned any German. At the orphanage, the nuns routinely gave her a nightgown to wear before bed, but the adoptive parents made little Teresa sleep in her undergarments at this rural homestead.

Did the Catholic nuns know that this new family did not like Jews? The new school environment was also frightening for Teresa. The children called her "a Jew" immediately (causing her to believe she was an outcast during those formative years).

As an adult, this adoptee speculated that she was intentionally sent to a German Catholic family by the Foundling Hospital sisters. Did her Jewish parents try to find her? Teresa remembered reading that "Catholic orphanages refused to return Jewish children to their parents." This triggered curiosity.

Eventually, Teresa wondered if she could get more answers if she traveled to the hospital. When she got there, it dawned on her that she was not the only orphan-train rider. She quietly accepted her life situation, but when a nun disclosed that they had placed 5,000 New York children into Kansas homes, Teresa no longer felt so isolated! She was not the only one!

As a senior citizen, she did attempt to politely retrieve her birth certificate, but she overhead a nun say, "Thank God, someone came back who was cheerful and didn't complain."

Teresa thought to herself: 'I could complain, too! My Schoenchen home wasn't the greatest. However, she said nothing aloud.'

Upon Teresa's death, she remained loyal to the Catholic Church and to the nuns despite never reuniting with her Jewish mother (nor was she given answers after inquiring about her). In the 1960s, and at the age of 73, she was told face-to-face: "Your case is closed." She had already heard this answer twice before. This was her last attempt.

Even as a toddler of four years, Teresa Bieker, adopted in 1910, opposed the idea of being given a new name. A priest tried to console her, claiming how lucky she was because not all her friends "got to be somebody's child." Meanwhile, she wondered, How will her mother find her if everyone called her by a different name?

***

"So, you're happy here." Mrs. Spallen made the sound like a statement, not a question.

If I say yes, nothing bad will happen, but if I say no, what will she do? Maybe tell Mrs. Bieker, who will slap me later. ...Yes." ~ Teresa Biecker, adopted in 1910

"Good."

Back to the Future

On June 15, 2014, The New York Times published an article, "New York Adoptees Fight for Access to Birth Certificates," echoing a complaint heard on forums from all over the Internet about antiquated adoption laws that date back to the 1930s. More and more of today's adopted people are compelled to unearth their ancestry for medical reasons, but, as one woman stated in the article, "My original birth certificate sits in a building in New York City, and I'm not entitled to it."

***

Excerpt from
"Mail Order Kids"
ADOPTION
What You Should Know

Adopted? Do you believe adoptees should have a right to their birth certificates and adoption documents? Link to adult adoptee survey. Or visit Adoption Truth & Transparency Worldwide Network on Facebook, or adoptiontruth.org.

"Adoption was built on the current foundation of crimes and lies and obvious coercion, but that kinder [...] gentler face of adoption was just remarketed, slicker, but just as coercive[,] if not more subtle and more deadly[,] because they had perfected the seduction."

Claudia Corrigan D'Arcy,
From the website Musings of the Lame

THEY CALLED US NEGATIVE[2]

Once in a while, I would run across online adoptee discussion groups where members confided (affectionately or repulsively) their memories of church potlucks where we really did drink Kool-Aid from plastic jugs on fields of yellow straw matted by station wagons, golden Cadillacs, and a fleet of recycled school buses. In the mid-to-late 1970s, I also remember horse-drawn wagon rides, potato-sack races, and rushing into giant haystacks to find tossed pennies. The very mention of these church picnics by fellow transracial adoptees immediately brought me back to attending church picnics and whatnot in the middle of nowhere during my upbringing. And for a good many of us, it was what most people would deem an all-American childhood.

---

[2] **Caution:** This chapter contains a disapproving critique of the adoption practice and might not be suitable for some readers. Discretion is advised. It contains investigative and whistle-blowing perspectives against the practice, revealing what some adult adoptees believe to be a violation of their human right to know and have access to their family. Skip to chapter "The True Self".

Everyone experiences their upbringing as normal and abnormal, and many of us do not stop to question our upbringing. Why should we? But, for various adoptees, we did not find ourselves in these better environments on our own accord. A great many adoptive parents did not ask if they could adopt us. And, unlike prearranged marriages, we were not old enough to fully understand the life-long aftermath, or approve of the legal contract. Many of us were sent to religious environments by adoption agencies owned, operated, or at least coordinated by evangelicals who self-proclaimed that they knew what was best for us. But, what about those of us who were never lost in the first place, nor "waiting to be adopted" as claimed on beautiful award-winning evangelical websites?

* * *

Today's Evangelical Orphan Movement (EOM) share numerous commonalities with The Peoples Temple of Disciples of Christ, which devolved into a pro-belief (at all costs) aftermath, prompting us to look at the personality traits specific to Reverend Jones—a seemingly respectable adoptive father, also a widely charismatic man who eventually guided his congregation to their deaths. What does today's EOM have in common with yesteryear's pastor? Especially when in the beginning, his movement all started innocently enough. The fundamentalist minister merely preached for his followers to separate from their families and join his church like any good preacher might advise.

However, Jim Jones led those devotees to their deaths years later. And, most of us know that his cult following resulted in one of the well-known massacres in US history.

So what does Jim Jones and the EOM have in common? Shockingly, you will discover that they have much in common. Because most of us have heard what happened in the case of Jim Jones, this prompted the examination into his life to pinpoint where exactly things went wrong. From this investigation, we can better protect individuals and families so that history does not repeat itself.

At least we can draw inspiration from the people who saved themselves from the massacre, including the Korean-born adoptee, Suzanne, who left her adoptive father's congregation and refused to return to Guyana in 1978 even after her adoptive mother begged her to go. (The transcript of the phone conversation is published in a forthcoming book tentatively titled: Master Adoption.)

* * *

At first, Jim Jones, born in 1931, and his wife, Marceline, appeared like a typical all-American family. While reading about Jones's personality, it seemed like almost anyone could have unconsciously fallen under his teachings or even risen to his level of power.

In fact, my adoptive father was born a year before Jim Jones, helping me to realize that he and my father could have easily been friends in their young adulthood and would have had a lot in common. Fortunately, despite being actively engaged in the church (like Jones had been), my adoptive father did not rise to such prominence—although as a "ruling church elder," an adult Sunday School teacher, Boy Scout Leader, choir director, he was prominent in the church setting, thus seemingly superman-esque from a child's point of view. Like those in Jonestown, any one of us can live under cult-like conditions, not even realize it, and of course, would deny such a statement. Thus, to see from a clarified perspective, we must consider detaching ourselves emotionally from our childhoods and see from what can be called a bird's eye view.

June of 1949, Jones married Marceline, a nursing student at the Trinity United Methodist Church. This man would become a born-again Christian, motivated mostly by the biblical ideal to "sell what we have and give it to the corporate community of our church," as he would later sermonize before Jonestown. As a fundamentalist under the veneer of a loving adoptive father, and a devoted minister, he assembled an expansive following, which would reach tens of thousands of listeners. Because of the racial disillusionment regarding the 1950s state of social and political affairs in the United States, Jones could easily attract potential members. In the beginning, no one suspected that the community Jim and his devoted wife formed would eventually fall from grace, later to commit one of the worst massacres in contemporary US history. Even today, few know that the crux of this fall occurred over a custody battle between the parents of a little boy that Reverend

Jim Jones aggressively claimed belonged to him. Hence the phrase: "drinking the Kool-Aid" came to be known as referring to someone who is so indoctrinated in a certain belief that there is a gullible (yet fierce) refusal to acknowledge that anything could be wrong with the circumstances. Surprisingly, the reverend flaunted a congregation for Christ of two million followers, spanning past the United States, down through South America and across Europe. Using photos of his rainbow family to prompt interest and collect donations, minister Jones also served as one of the most active and ardent campaigners for intercountry, transracial, and domestic adoptions. He believed he must introduce the world's children to Christ (or at least save one, two, or more), and that it was unfair to them if he didn't. As a consequence of such an attitude, Pastor Jones unknowingly spearheaded what is called "Orphan Fever" today. The root cause of adoption trafficking, according to many informed and aware political groups led by adopted people who feel obligated to shine a light on certain violations.

What does Jim Jones have to do with the EOM today? Since his thoughts, beliefs, and teachings were proclaimed to be on the right side of God, the ministry permitted him authority over the lives of other people's children. Those who contested his self-appointed righteousness were perceived as not fully immersed and called negative and ungrateful. We see this type of treatment against anyone who dares to question religious leaders all over the world wide web today. Similarly, questioners of adoption practices are ousted entirely from political and social dialogue.

Like some fundamentalists of yesteryear, Jones claimed that he (and he alone) could speak on behalf of God. This claim of his created a messianic savior-like reputation for himself. He deceptively recruited followers who later left all that they knew and isolated themselves from listening to concerns voiced by their families. The followers were then convinced by the notion that Reverend Jones could protect them from the immoral members of a secular society. Feedback was only valued if given by other members of the congregation—the more devoted, the more moral the member. If a member questioned the beliefs of its leader or his devotees, the questioners were convinced that something was inherently wrong with them. (You will see this poor treatment against adoptees take place regularly in groups led by religious adoptive parents.)

In June of 1952, Jones began his illustrious career as a Methodist student pastor in Indianapolis and, while there, also attended a Pentecostal Church. In 1954, he opened a church of his own and immediately tried to increase membership as many ministers did at that time. The Community Unity Church was based on core Methodist and charismatic Pentecostal sects. In 1955, he was able to purchase a building for the church named "Wings of Deliverance, Inc." On February 5th, 1956, he became an ordained minister in the Independent Assemblies of God. He then became an ordained minister affiliated with the Disciples of Christ denomination and changed the name to the "Peoples Temple Full Gospel Church," supported by his devoted wife, associate pastors, a secretarial board, and its planning commission. Because of his friendship with and acceptance of Blacks during a time of turmoil and racism across the United States, Jones reached out to African-American communities, and to South America. Reverend Jones continued to preach about integration and racial equality and, like several leaders of his time, advocated for his congregation to adopt children from various backgrounds to demonstrate racial tolerance. Of course, being the first to adopt, he served as a shining example, providing proof that his church was not racist.

The minister and his wife adopted seven children domestically, transracially, and internationally. The first child the Jones placed under their wings was a nine-year-old female named Agnes, who first wandered up to the church entrance after one of Rev. Jones' sermons in 1954 and gave him a handful of violets while stuttering the words, "I love you." The young girl immediately won the hearts of the minister and his wife. Rumors claimed that Agnes was "Native American and the daughter of a prostitute." When she was eleven-years-old, the girl's mother allowed the Joneses to adopt her.

In October of 1958, Jones traveled to California to pick up two Korean children: a four-year-old girl and a two-year-old boy. Like many adoptive parents, he and his wife proudly fell in love with their war orphans. Another fellow evangelist handed Jim Jones the two children on a stage of all places and broadcasted worldwide. I supposed that's how the good people of the world adopted in those days.[3]

Jones then passed on his goodness to his people, like any good minister would do. He had been encouraging members of his congregation to adopt children, especially young orphans in war-ravaged Korea. The Joneses themselves set the example. The idea that adopting could possibly be a racist act or another form of colonialism and imperialism, or that sixty years into the future adopted people would point out the fact that they never signed the contract that bound them to such authorities, would have astounded him. If he was still alive, no doubt he would be writing letters in major evangelical online newspapers, attacking adopted people or concerned relatives, accusing all of having an infatuation with blood-ties, and part of the evil "anti-this or that" camp as if we are the mentally-ill ones unable to bond.

In fact, today's EOM is still directed by numerous preaching adoptive fathers from around the western world, and it is not uncommon to see an identical "savior complex" and "orphan fever" attitude prevail, requiring congregational members to submit to certain threatening, yet loving sermons. If you listen and abide, you will be rewarded; If you do not submit, you risk everlasting damnation.

---

[3] *Adoptopia: The Life and Times of Adoptive Father, the Reverend Jim Jones* (and infamous cult leader) includes a historical re-enactment based from a FBI audio transcript archived at "Alternative Considerations of Jonestown and Peoples Temple," sponsored by the Special Collections of Library and Information Access at San Diego State University.

However, there are a couple differences between Jim Jones' "savior complex" fiasco and the EOM's "orphan fever": In Jim Jones's case, his followers actually got to choose whether or not they wanted to be a member of his church. In the EOM case, the chosen children are not given any right to choose to be sent to adoption culture. On top of that, their identity is completely deleted by the adoption facilitator. This means that if the child wanted to return, they would no longer have the information about their biological families to locate them—even into adulthood. In fact, the intention of intercountry and domestic adoption and the way the child welfare programs had been set up, "adoptees" were (and still are) stigmatized so much so that they are not allowed to be given such information—even into their elder years. Instead, the adopted and required to submit and devote ourselves to an evangelistic higher authority, consisting of threatening rhetoric, and no support for the adopted due to the willful ignorance of compliant devotees.

In the case of adoption culture, still today, "non-believers" are treated poorly and punished. It would not be surprising at all to watch the EOM leaders and their devotees refuse to acknowledge the fact that they have separated families or inflicted any type of hurt. Instead, we can expect to be continuously ridiculed, name-called, and labeled weak, sinful, obsessed with blood-ties, or whatever kneejerk and insulting name they will come up with next. Their crusade has become our crisis.

Excerpts from Adoption Books for Adults

***

Excerpt from
"A Surprise Promoter of Adoption"
ADOPTOPIA
A Deep Dive into the Life and Times of Adoptive
Father, the Reverend Jim Jones

***

"Fallible and discouraging thoughts will eventually deconstruct and come to an end. Such evolution is the succession of nature. The only constant in life is evolution (and evolution equals truth). Lao-Tzu's principles suggest that the highest state of humankind starts by changing how we think about what it means to be intelligent. By doing so, we protect ourselves from intruders armed with their agenda for our lives."

~Janine Myung Ja,
Master Adoption:
Claim Your Authentic Power

THEY CALLED US
UNGRATEFUL

Have you ever been asked to imagine what your life would have been like if you were not adopted? The intention of this is to convince you that you are truly lucky. You are to imagine that if you had not been adopted, you would have died of starvation or ended up a street beggar or, if you are a female, you would be a prostitute, of course. You are supposed to appreciate the facilitator's arrangement for your life—as if they, alone, work for God. Many of us, at one time or another, have had the implication made regarding the luck of our adoption, and if not already, it is only a matter of time. When I first requested my adoption records, Molly Holt, the biological daughter of Harry and Bertha Holt, asked me to reflect upon what my life would have been like had I not been adopted. She failed to tell me that mothers had been counseled into relinquishing, and families were rejected from agencies when they returned for their children. No

65

one from their end told me poverty-stricken families could not afford to attend adoption conferences sponsored by agencies and, as a consequence, ousted from the property when they inquired about their missing children. In this particular line of business, requests made by potentially loving parents (of loss) are routinely and swiftly brushed off by those in navy blue suits, as if no big deal.

At this point in adoption history, most if not all, adoption healing books on the market have been written by adoptive parents—adoptive parents who tend to place the blame on adoptees whenever problems occur. *Adopters* tend not to look within themselves to ask what toxic attitudes and behaviors they could change to advocate for our truth and transparency. So, if you are an adopted person, and you feel disempowered, I suggest that books written by adoptive parents might not give you credit and the benefit of the doubt that books written by your peers would. For example, I doubt that many adoptive parents will tell you that you have the right to disagree with them and that all humans have the right to know the truth about one's biology, or at the very least, have access to one's true identity. Instead, some *adopters* are prone to accuse adoptees of having Reactive Attachment Disorder (RAD). They even force adoptees to see psychiatrists or specialists as if the children are reacting unnaturally to loss. Then the child must cope with the side effects of prescription medicine. Of course, we do tend to bond with adoptive parents and family, for it is instinctive for us to adapt, especially after being placed in a situation where we are influenced solely by the adoptive community and not given a choice in the matter. The affection we give as children is genuine. The care and concern we give to the people within the realm of our adoptive placements are genuine gifts. But just because we give this affection freely does not mean we should ignore our own needs, rights, and justice.

I no longer fall for the adoptive parent's short-sightedness, which tends to blame adopted children for failing to bond with their adoptive families like we see in many self-help books written by *adopters*. Reactive Attachment Disorder (RAD) is really a natural reaction for anyone who has been sent without consent to foreign territory, whether an unfamiliar home across the street or a foreign nation. In my opinion, every human being would have a difficult time bonding, let alone adjusting to the rules of the unknown terrain. Yet, young children are expected to immediately bond? I believe, as small children, we innately knew we should not be forced to bond with strangers. If we did not adapt so eagerly and easily, those are perfectly natural reactions when placed in unfamiliar situations. The child's surprise and shock should be expected. Do we expect any other group of people to immediately place their lives in the hands of strangers? *No!* Thus, wouldn't it be fair to assume that a lack of immediate bonding is natural? That it could be our body's instinct to protect itself. Instead of diagnosing the child of having RAD, let's see the situation for what it is: The child is reacting naturally. Maybe instead of suffering from RAD, we could call this instinct, ANR: *A Natural Reaction.* There. Now we are no longer radical with some sort of disorder.

We are human beings like everyone else. We are multi-dimensional beings. We should not be reduced to a label such as *anti-this* or *anti-that*[4]. We are sons, daughters, sisters, brothers, parents, aunts, uncles, grandparents, cousins, nephews, nieces, and grandchildren. We were born into a family web—a long thread of belonging to those of us before us and after us, and this link goes on and on for generations. In other words, no one is an orphan. All of us belong to a forever family—an everlasting line of DNA much grander than we could ever imagine. Every single human is a sacred being, and each of us belongs to a procession of sacred beings that go on from generations past to generations forward. Shouldn't all humans have access to their people? —Even people adopted?

When adopted children rebel against the placement, the child is responding naturally. Therefore, the individual should not be diagnosed with a disorder, nor given drugs to force the child to adapt and abide. At a collective level, those of us adopted know we should have the same rights as all other humans, and we have the right to disagree with those who engineered the modern mail-order system as if adoption, in industry-speak, is "as natural as giving birth."

Of course, the vast majority of us have acclimated by now that we are adults, and the love

---

[4]It is not uncommon for people adopted to be labeled *anti-adoption, anti-Christian* and even *anti-God* when advocating for access to our original birth certificate, access to adoption documents, or upon searching for birth family.

we give is very real. Yet, to be fair to all involved, we need to consider that adoption is *not* as natural as giving birth. To put it bluntly, we adopted people are perceptive. What if those who separated us were the ones who had trouble bonding? Is not claiming that if they had not removed us from a "sinful" and "backward" country (as if bad and dangerous compared to their angelic safe havens), operating from a fear-based belief system?

To protect our people, we must be aware of those who have exploited generations past. Now that we have survived being "saved," adopted people deserve to have a say about such schemes that appear sweet on the surface. As more and more of us find our families, we are discovering that we were not sent to "better" people, we were merely sent to different people—all people face challenges. Every family has its peculiarities, and that is fine. But in adoption, our personal boundaries have been crossed. As my sister points out, it would be completely unethical and immoral to issue new identities onto institutionalized elders, and then send them overseas to foreign nations to be cared for. To anyone with ethics and morals, such an idea is an absolute "no, no," crossing personal boundaries. Off-limits. Yet, the adoptioneers (pioneers of adoption profiteering) of years past have legally profited from the global market—targeting children who were unable to articulate their thoughts about the situation and groomed to love their placements.

The industry is built on the overall assumption that the applying *adopters* are "loving" and "good" while the biological family is "sinful" or bad. It is so easy to blame the victims—especially when the victims are conveniently hidden. Without knowledge or permission from that of our immediate and extended family members, including both parents, thousands of children are continuously exported and documented as if "orphaned" despite having living families. I call this false advertising. The mother is isolated so that it is easier to convince her of her inadequacies. In other scenarios, the mothers are led to believe that since the pregnancy was unplanned, they should immediately relinquish. Then the facilitators go on to lead paying customers to assume that the children are unwanted and unloved. The truth of the matter? The parents were never given a chance to parent, nor were they given ethical counseling, which encouraged and empowered them to do so. It has become normalized and part of the global culture to suggest adoption even by those who do not profit from the trade, without really understanding the life-long consequences of the act upon the infant/child, the parents, the siblings, immediate and extended family members.

Instead, laws have been passed for strangers across the globe to be able to legally obtain babies. This standardization has been the special interest group's covert tactic to be able to obtain children without having to document and contend with their parents. It was not until the 1950s when the profiteers began giving directions —telling native citizens specific locations to leave their children— under the guise of child protection and welfare.

Why do I say "master adoption"? Adoption has mastered not only the world's perspective on child welfare but also violated the personal boundaries and the sacred space of children from every creed and culture. Just take a look at the numbers: "Updated Research: 13 BILLION $$$ in Profits in the Adoption Industry."[5]

On the other hand, we were never told of our rights—and that is what is wrong with this industry. It is not in the adoption profiteers self-interest to do so. So, in an attempt to protect vulnerable mothers, families, and fellow adopted people, it is up to us to be informed.

As you probably know, by this point in its history, adoption is assumed to be a charitable act—something glorified. In the past, fierce marketing movements by religious leaders and agency facilitators attracted more applicants to the practice. At the time of the setup, families of loss and indigenous communities were not given the opportunity to provide input about how the laws were set up. This way, more and more affluent people could afford to build their families without giving much thought to those left behind.

Since the inception of the practice, success stories were passed from church to church and social event to social event. Adoption was only shown in a positive light by religious groups, mostly various churches, and then broadcast by satellite to the contemporary televangelists and stadium preachers. Small children and teenagers were taught that our role was to be seen and not heard. This immediate acceptance allowed religious authorities to grant

[5]http://www.adoptionbirthmothers.com/adoption-industry-13-billion-in-profits/

71

themselves the power to move more children without argument. Those who argued were scolded and accused of whining or complaining. To question authority's methods was simply inconceivable for most children trained to behave and honor their elders. Such obedience included giving unquestionable respect toward newly assigned adoptive parents. Many of our biological parents were stigmatized as inadequate and incapable of loving their children. And we were caught in the middle—left to pretend we were orphaned or forced to juggle two families while ignoring our own rights.

Putting politics aside, we have become independent and even rebellious souls. We tend to take the bull by the horns and lead ourselves. Your awareness into the land of adoption and evolutionary process through it, will take us into the future, advocating for innate human rights. We, as a unified collective, can make history together, if we so wish. *If you're tired of that annoying question: "Have you ever thought about what your life would have been like if you were not adopted."* Maybe, we would not have been prostitutes, beggars, or homeless. Maybe we would have been well fed, educated (or an educator), and famous, like Confucius, Siddhartha Gautama, or Lao-tzu. Maybe it is time to deconstruct adoption, so that we can see it for what it is.

***

Excerpt from
"That Annoying Question"
MASTER ADOPTION
Claim Your Authentic Power

THE TRUE SELF

REMEMBER THAT OL' SCHOOLYARD chant, "Sticks and Stones will break my bones, but words will never hurt me"? Actually, it's a lie. Yes, sticks and stones can break bones, but words are also capable of hurting humanity. In fact, words can break the will, and joy of a person, and this turmoil can be passed down for many generations. Words like sinful have been used since the inception of the human language to uplift and tear down individuals, clans, communities, and even entire countries. There probably isn't a human on earth who has not been reduced to a label or called something offensive. This can have a hurtful influence on the self-worth— in fact, more than we might be aware—because words are energy.

When it comes to the conscious awareness of the true self, the great Western thinkers of today are aligning with three well-known Eastern philosophers. Even Albert Einstein, a proponent of Eastern Philosophy, recognized the value and sacredness of nature when he said, "Look deep into nature, and then you will understand everything better." Words Are Energy, and the energy system aligns with the great thinkers of the East.

Confusion can come from being deprived of the truth, and for people adopted, the truth of who we are is our true nature. Adopted people have the additional burden of secrets, sealed documents, and assumptions made against our origin. Even though Dr. Maltz Maxwell, M.D., did not focus on adopted people in his studies, he wrote about self-perception in his book, Psycho-Cybernetics. He said, "To deal effectively with a problem, you must have some understanding of its true nature. Most of our failures in human relations are due to 'misunderstandings.'"

Even popular modern-day psychologists (despite being unknowledgeable of the human rights concerns of adopted people and families of loss) are becoming aware of the "authentic self," otherwise known as our innate nature. In an article on Oprah.com, Dr. Phil wrote, "Your persona should be congruent with your core self. He called the true nature the authentic self, referring to it as a beach ball. It does not matter how much we try to hold it down; it will eventually try to pop back up to the water's surface. This is the nature of our authentic self. He went onto explain, "It's draining to bury your authentic self—and it's a losing battle. Remember when you were a kid, and you tried to hold a beach ball underwater, but inevitably it would pop back up? Then you'd push it back down and fight it until it slipped up once again. Doing that all day would be exhausting, but that's essentially what's happening when you're constantly trying to deny who you are".

From his book, *Self Matters,* Dr. McGraw also shared how it felt to be incongruent when he was younger, "Like an enemy I knew as intimately as any friend, I came to know the nagging, constant emptiness of the incongruent life. I ignored myself and lived for people, purposes, and goals that weren't my own. I betrayed who I was and instead accepted a fictional substitute that was defined from the outside in."

Many intercountry adoptees report being groomed to ignore and even disrespect the true nature of the self. The foreign-born adopted child might have been instructed to abide by authorities who were armed with an agenda and needed to exert control, thus benefited and polished up the practice of adoption, and raised the reputation of the adoption agencies, allowing for more access to children, but did little to consider the unique needs of the child adopted from overseas long after the transaction.

What is the true nature? I highlight the philosophies of individuals from yesterday and today's Eastern and Western culture, each of whom provided insight into the true nature of the human spirit, which can be used as examples for those of us who are deprived of our birth philosophy and culture.

In Eastern Philosophy, it is believed that all people make up the collective; every individual, no matter what the position, is a vital member of the energetic realm. Even though we as humans might not be able to see our value or even sense this invisible network, we are members of the universal oneness through our spirituality and our divine energy. Disconnecting from the false self (influenced and shaped by others) is a process that involves tuning into our true nature what I like to sometimes refer to as Sacred Energy Life Force (S.E.L.F.). Through respite and restoration, we can access the true self where empathy resides and empower our mindset to be receptive to the universal self that connects us to all that is.

Eastern Philosophy is not considered a religion because it does not threaten people to believe in one certain way or risk being sent to hell, but is based on the realistic and apparent laws of nature: for every action, there is a reaction. Life is not for us to judge—in fact, judging causes pain—but to observe from a place of calm, solidarity, and truth. Rooted in this foundation, we are able to accomplish whatever needs to be accomplished. We are better empowered. The following three Eastern philosophers, Lao-Tzu, the Buddha, and Confucius, were aware of the true nature found within, and they are the individuals I focused on in my investigation.

Lao Tzu said, "Recognizing the cycle of life is enlightenment; ignoring it leads to disaster." We can interpret this to mean conscious awareness of one's true nature, and the connection with oneness assists in the discovery of the power and strength of the spirit, as well as the greatness within all of humanity. In doing so, we find that all are related to what is called the Source of All. The words Taoism, The Way of Nature, Connection with the Mother of the Universe, God-Mind, or Divine Oneness have all been used by various schools of thought in reference to the True Nature.

***

Excerpt from
"Modern Realizations"
*ONE ADOPTEE * THREE WISE MEN*[6]

---

[6]This chapter and the following chapter contain excerpts from books that do not focus on adoption, but rather uplifting ideas and suggestions that could pertain to anyone.

WHAT IF WE CAME FROM THE STARS?

Remember that old insult, "Go back to where you came from?" On the first day of seventh grade, I got the message thrown at me from a busload of elementary-age school kids. But it wasn't until my mid-twenties before I found a philosophy that gave me back to my true self—at least a remnant. The result? Humanism is a great thing. In the home I grew up in and when unable to travel, I enjoyed the wisdom of my ancestors by exploring several philosophies formerly off-limits like Taoism and Buddhism. Today, I am excited and proud of who I am and from where I originate. I love the narratives of all nations; each culture is a collective of wisdom and insight rooted in a profound history of strength and willpower, making the framework of the human will to get up and rise from the dread and everyday drudgery that life can sometimes, surprisingly, bring on. This expansion of philosophy is the motivation for the book.

As a consequence of additional learning from the philosophy of my birth culture, I believe there is no such thing as an illegitimate birth. ...Since being displaced from Seoul in 1972, I feel as if my life has been pulled to revert to my natural self—but whatever that was, I didn't know. Today, at middle-age, I accept the things I cannot change and take action on the things I can. As a result, the best thing to do when faced with people who can't see you is to identify and appreciate yourself. For me, this means finding value in my sacred energy life force, a place from which all of life originates.

At the very least, we were planned by the stars. (What could be better than that?)

***

If you have ever been removed from or deprived of your family, a circle of friends, coworkers, or even a beloved community, you probably know how uncertain it can feel to be a bit lonely. Our saving grace becomes our return to oneness. Sometimes leaving our childhood teachings is the best thing we can do for ourselves; we can use this as an opportunity to remember from where we originate and become ourselves fully. I believe that all of us humans are birthed from the Universe. They may claim that we are "orphans," but we are born to two individuals who belong to an extensive line of maternal and paternal lineage, aunts, uncles, and cousins, who spring forth nieces, and nephews. When feeling heavy energy, it helps me to remember that I belong to a universal family line, and not only that, my ancestry is stretched throughout time and everlasting. In fact, it's universal. We come from the stars. Together we exist. Apart from that, we are a great invisible family.

This long ancestry makes us part of a unique global clan. We might feel alone at times, but from behind the scenes, we are surrounded by essences much larger than we can imagine. This lineage is in our blood, and it is in our chi (our breath of life). It lives in us. We live in it. We are the extension of it: a significant member of this everlasting thread of heritage planned (and planted by Mother Nature and Father Time). Some on the earth plane might preach our birth was somehow sinful or an accident, but such is not the case. We were planned by the highest and greatest and fiercest of forces. We might not see who we truly are on the surface, but each human matters—not just a saintly few who claim to be closest to God.

Your physical life is meaningful and valuable, even if you just sit there. You are one of the creators. You, along with your ancestral body of relatives, coordinated your life in conjunction with the lives of those around you, and all of life springs outward from there. You might not be aware of your life's purpose and the details that go into that, but the pieces of the puzzle will eventually fit together, and the grand scheme of things shall be presented. We, given our limited perspectives, might not grasp the value of our own life, and there is a possibility that some of us might never be told all of the truth about our value. However, every step we take is sacred, even if we believe we are taking steps backward. We will reach our destination whether or not we believe in it, or in ourselves, or the greater oneness of all there is or God itself. We will reach the destination planned by the unmanifested Source. It is not a matter of if; it is a matter of when. The question is, how are we going to walk the journey?

We, earthlings, have two choices. We can walk it veiled from our worth, or we can walk in awareness. How will you walk? That is the question. Whatever you decide, you are loved. Loved by an endless ancestral family that knows no boundaries.

From an expansive point of view—one that spans time and space (including life between lives), our ancestral family wanted us so much—desperately wanted us in the picture—desperately wanted to acknowledge us and to be acknowledged. The problem is that humankind is unwilling to see beyond the surface at times. Sometimes fear and doubt are the enemies. It is fear and doubt that reject our bloodlines, ousts them from the conversation, and made up stories about them. And the rest of the parishioners believed these stories as if they needed for us to be someone we didn't want to be. Our ancestors had the same problem when they walked the earth. Proselytizers insisted that our people were worthless, sinful creatures! It is our time to defend this from happening to future generations. It's our time now.

When you stand for humankind, proselytizers might hate you for it. They might blame you. They might accuse you of wrongdoing. They might do everything in their power to prove you wrong and reduce you down to someone you are not to make them look good, to fluff up their feathers, to prove that their way is the right way to prove that they are right and righteous. Those against humanity wish for us to be afraid. When we are afraid and filled with shame, there is a tendency to stay nonchalant and less likely to begin toward our right back to self.

Few had the guts to stand on behalf of our ancestors! Communication lines were cut and severed, ancestors were abandoned, excluded from the dialogue. They want you to know that you are loved. Deeply loved. Loved so much that there is nothing you could do to break this love. They can see you for who you truly are. What if we weren't born in sin?

What if we belong to something vast and spectacular? What if we come from the stars? What if each of us is the missing link in our own lives—and the lives of those before us? What if our ancestors are proud of us? And they were proud of who they were during their own lives centuries past? They fought the good fight for our existence, and they did good. Yes, today, many modern conveniences distract us from identifying and recognizing the miraculous and capable tribe from which we are descendants.

Imagine that your ancestors want you to know that there is more to you than meets the eye. Your ancestors hold you in high regard. They love you. You are their prodigal son/daughter. They are impatiently waiting for your return, for the great family reunion. Your ancestors are on your side— always on your side. Whatever you decide to do, your ancestors support you one hundred percent. They truly believe in you; they trust that you will be kind and empathetic to all people.

All humans originate from the stars, and we have the Universe within us. We were planned (and planted) by something larger and grander than ever imagined. We were planned with all of us in mind—the human tribe—the oneness of human nature.[7]

GOING BACK TO ZEN
Where to Find Peace so You can Live Like Mad
by Rev. Dr. Janine Vance, Ph.D. Philosophy

---

[7] This chapter is also located in the ebook *Going Back to Zen: Where to Find Peace so You Can Live in Peace*.

GRATITUDE

It's been almost 25 years since I first started my researching journey into the land of adoption. Discovering the good, the bad, and the ugly along the way has been a roller coaster ride of many ups and downs. I need to thank you for taking the time to read these excerpts from my entire collective. When it comes to adoption, these snapshots are the mere tip of the iceberg.

I need to thank my husband for supporting me for more than 32 years now. He worked at the same job one month short of 30 years before the company closed the doors in our area, and he was laid off. But, the timing was somehow synchronized with the greater good. The job loss allowed him to travel back to Vietnam in time to see his mom before she passed away.

One of my husband's favorite sayings throughout our marriage is "if we're not enough without it, we'll never be enough with it." This means that if we focus on appreciating who we are at the core and all that

that includes, we won't need more to make us happy. If we're not satisfied with who we are now, even the fancy bells and whistles will not satisfy us. Wanting and needing is known in Eastern thought to be the cause of suffering. Non-judgment, or a neutral balanced perspective, cures that suffering.

I met my husband in the late 1980s. At age fourteen he was instructed to leave Vietnam, his birthplace, and head toward Malaysia. He courageously left his homeland alone—without the help of his parents. Sadly, that was the last time he saw his father.

Sometimes I think of my husband like an Aquaman because he has so much confidence on the water. This is due to regularly swimming and boating when a teenager for the customers at his parents' cafe. Then once he arrived in the states, he was hired on as a fisherman in the gulf of Mexico and continued to expertly navigate rough waters.

I started dating him after that job (and ever since), he has supported us throughout all these decades at a manual labor job so I could fulfill my insatiable curiosity and continue a never-ending writing hobby.

I really resonate with taking care of those closest to us in the best way possible and a big believer in the benefits of that. It really worked out for us. I've been fortunate to have my husband's help for those decades so we could provide care for dad inside our home. As I have mentioned in other books, in 1984, my he fell 100 feet while hang-gliding (when I was age twelve years old) and suffered a traumatic brain injury that left him permanently disabled. He lost the house he designed and built due to the disability (since his wife/my mom died after I graduated from high school).

I also need to thank my twin sister for these years. She and my dad have always been my number one fans. While He helped me edit numerous books, she has given me 100% emotional support and has financially donated funds toward my writing career throughout the years. Her family, along with my two daughters (I can't believe they're adults already!), have uplifted me throughout my endless endeavor to investigate, write, and share. I'm very proud of the people who are closest to me. Today, my twin is a frontline worker at the nursing home's sister building, Life Care, the first hit by COVID-19. She truly felt it was her responsibility to continue working for the elders in her care regardless of how dangerous it all felt like when the virus first appeared, especially at the very beginning. Her sense of duty never wavered, even though it put her health and even potentially her life at risk.

Sadly, 2020 has been a devastating year for many of us around the world. November of last year, my dad began showing signs of dementia, and I could no longer provide care for him. Previously, for my entire life, we've had many great daily discussions. As a consequence, he became a good friend. To lose him as a daily confidant has been challenging, and then not to be able to see him for numerous months due to the virus left me grieving. Adding to the turmoil was learning that after Dad had been released from the hospital for aftercare and therapy, he was physically abused for six months at a nursing home since family members are not permitted to visit. It pains me to see his remaining years have ended in loss, trauma, and grief. Unbelievably, Dad turned 90 on Nov 13th.

Today, I think it's a miracle that he lived 36 years after that initial hang gliding accident in the early '80s. None of us believed that he would live this long! He not only survived a traumatic brain injury that left him permanently disabled, but he recently survived physical punches and numerous unexplained bodily bruises from a nursing home staff member. Devastatingly, compounded by dementia and even delirium at times, he is unable to communicate his wishes and needs at all.

Dad supported my entire 20 plus-year writing hobby. I believe we had a soul contract to shed light on the crisis of adoption trafficking. He always gave me his full attention whenever I walked into the room. He was a continuous staunch supporter of my work and of Against Child Trafficking and for the rights of all people—especially adoptees—to search for our birth families if we wished. He even suspected that he might have lost his own newborn daughter to that secretive underground network of Catholic priests, nuns, doctors, and nurses who lied about stillborn babies to traffic them for adoption profits. (More than 350,000 missing children were found, according to an investigation.)

I do believe Dad suffered from a lot of losses and turmoil throughout his life. I'd like to ensure that Dad gets palliative and comfort care that would cover grief relief for trauma victims. Today, he has a difficult time articulating his wishes and needs. If I were to really imagine a miracle, I'd like for him to live out the rest of his life in the house that he designed and built (but lost due to his disability). This would be his dream come true.

ALLEN VANCE 1930 - 2021

According to a survey by adult adoptees, thus far (December 2020), 100% believe the adoption contract should no longer be between only the applicants and the facilitator but should also include the child's signature. (Makes sense to me.) Because, numerous adoptees have said, it is the "adoptee" who lives the consequence of adoption.

Because sweeping generalizations are made that assume all adopted children are sent to what's labeled in adoption culture as "better families," the laws refuse to recognize that tricking, counseling, coercing, or abducting your child for overseas shipment to a foreign nation is *child trafficking*— even if your child is sent to a pedophile, abused, or murdered. Even though families of loss carry additional burdens their entire lives, authorities can use the legal adoption system to deport your child overseas, and it is not understood as "exploitive," but rather "in the child's best interest." Consequently, adoption laws do not fully protect children, families separated by adoption, or parents of loss, but rather justify, legalize, and regulate the transaction.

Adoption law is not a human right measure. Adoption laws ignore your innate right to each and every one of your biological family members—not just "birth mom," but also a connection with all your potential siblings. Instead of promoting or refining adoption laws, the most effective safety measure that we can encourage is the recognition of equal rights for all people—even for adopted people— which is ignored in adoption law.

While adoption profiteers, special-interest groups, and lobbyists fiercely fight for the *right to adopt*, we can also recognize the perspectives of numerous adoptees who no longer have legal permission to know or have access to their biological family because of the applicants' "right to adopt". Our civil liberties are recognized in the United Nations' Conventions and Declarations. These rights are inborn, innate, and of nature (God and/or Mother Nature—whatever you call the higher power) by birth. When it comes to protecting local and global families against child trafficking, let's advocate for equal rights and recovery.

*Catholic Mass Grave Sites of 350,800 Missing Children Found in Ireland, Spain, Canada | Global Adoption News (adoptionland.org)

ON WRITING

Ten questions Janine answers about writing and what she learned about researching adoption from the inside out.

***

1.
WHY DID YOU WRITE THIS SERIES OF BOOKS?

Writing is never about making money. Writing is about getting the truth out of your system before you die, and you need to be willing to spend your lifeblood to get the story told. If you cannot live without getting a certain truth out, then the work that goes into writing might not be worth it for you. So, the best gift to give any writer is just maybe recommending the book to a friend and sending them a link.

***

2.
WHAT SUGGESTIONS DO YOU HAVE FOR WANT-TO-BE AUTHORS?

If you ever decide to write a memoir, it might be one of the most difficult things you'll ever do (to yourself) especially in this day and age. Let me explain: I started writing in 1997, the day after my mom died. I had no writing training or experience, and was pretty much armed with only a high school diploma and I wasn't even a very good student to tell you the truth. I just dug myself deeper and deeper into the writing hole and gave myself hell while doing so. I could barely write a decent sentence, let alone a paragraph. I would go over every single sentence at least a million times over trying to restructure words into better sentences. I mulled over every paragraph, then each chapter: arranging, rearranging, tearing them apart, rebuilding them, hating them (and hating myself for being such a shitty writer, and making the whole thing harder on myself than need be), but eventually leaving those damn passages in the book because I had had enough! I could barely look at the words any longer. So, even after 20 years of starting this, not even I am satisfied with the finished result!! Just ask my daughters. Yesterday, I had asked them if I should rearrange the whole book again for the umpteenth time. They simply said, "No.") So if you didn't like how this whole thing turned out, I understand (even though I hope you do). I get it.

So you can no longer spend time fixated on getting this perfected or that perfected, because there's no such thing as perfection — unless you have a team of editors and a pocketful of cash to throw at people to do everything for you. But who has that? Only the top five percent! But history should be written by the people, for the people. You have to be willing to invest in yourself. When it came to writing in my case, I invested everything I had into the project and it became a lifelong endeavor to keep giving, giving, and giving.

**

3.
HOW LONG DID IT TAKE YOU TO WRITE AMERICANIZED '72?

It took a while. A long while. While living out this writing torture in my head throughout these 20+ years, I was able to raise two great daughters and I've been supported by a great guy since 1988. To say that I am exhausted is an understatement. If it were not for their understanding and patience, none of these books would have been written. Their allowance is the reason my books exist. Americanized '72 is my book retold and updated from a previous first version called Twins Found in a Box: Adapting to Adoption published in 2003. I've written more than ten books now and probably nine screenplays. (Of course, doesn't mean I like one or two of them, although I do believe all are of value and meaningful.) I have written in every genre and every single one of them will put you through a long difficult learning process. At least I can tell you now what NOT to do.

**

4.
WHAT'S THE HARDEST PART ABOUT WRITING A BOOK?

When you write your story, you will put your heart and soul out there for public judgment, and readers might respond with a "ho-hum," or "it was decent," or "she needs to be more positive," or "she needs to be more negative." You will never make everyone happy, and you'll be lucky if you can get one or two readers who actually love the book. Criticism is totally understandable, because, of course, no one sees the blood, sweat, tears, and years that turn into decades, that turn into two decades, and so on and so forth, all while just trying to figure this shit puzzle out. Nobody knows that you've slaved over the computer for so many years that now your eyes are almost completely worn out. In my case, the doctor told me my eyes were "sunburned." At my last optometrist appointment, she said it appeared as if somebody had scrubbed my eyeballs with sandpaper. Doesn't help that I am legally blind in one eye, also. All I can say about that is that at least I have one halfway decent eye. All I know is that I am in dire need to get all these books finished before my sight goes totally blurry and I can't see anything at all.

***

5.
WHAT'S YOUR CITIZENSHIP STATUS NOW?

In like, 1998, or so, my sister and I did apply for citizenship, paid the fees, waited and waited, got called upon, took the test, went through the interview process, and got naturalized. During the interview, I was asked if I had ever voted here in the states. "No," was my truthful answer. (Even though I was raised to believe and truly believed I was a US

Citizen and should vote, I never did. Maybe it had something to do with assuming that my voice doesn't matter.) The officer told me, "Good." Because if I had, he went on to explain, I would have been at risk of deportation. Great. I thought. I didn't even know where Korea was on the map at that time.

***

6.
HAVE YOU EVER BEEN TO KOREA?

The good news is that since becoming a citizen, I've been able to travel back to Korea three times. If you want, you can read about our short two week adventure in my book, The Search for Mother Missing: A Peek Inside International Adoption.) It's not a saga, like this book, just a short trip.

***

7.
DO YOU BELIEVE IN THE ADOPTION HAPPILY EVER AFTER STORY TODAY?

So, in the end, after all is said and done, I'm not sure if I believe in fairytale stories. At least not for me and my family, anymore. My adoption was about hard work and trying to give as much as you can while you're making it work. As you might know, Dad lived with me since Mom died. We spent years helping each other out. He was admitted to the hospital a few months ago, and now in a nursing home. After 20+ years of seeing each other: Every. Single. Day, while he lived with my family, I haven't been allowed to see him for almost two months now in the nursing home because of the coronavirus. Due to dementia, he is confused over why I am not visiting. The grief over the loss of his ability to articulate his needs (and me at his side to interpret his wishes), confusion over being given psychiatric drugs at the hospital (something he would be totally against because he had never taken anything more than aspirin as needed when he lived with me), and anxiety of the unknown, he is alone and in turmoil, which makes me feel helpless over his situation. Last I saw him, he was sobbing, reached out for me, and cried, "My company is dead." (He meant to say, my family is dead.) He started doing a ton of sit ups on the bed to make himself stronger so he could, as he said, "Go back to work at Boeing." I know he believes he needs to do something to help us all. He will be 90 this year.

Since I am no longer allowed to be at his side, he thinks I've abandoned him and I can't explain to him why I am not allowed to visit due to increasing dementia. He is unable to use a cell phone due to poor hand dexterity and lack of ability to focus. I wanted to be with him when he transitioned to the other side. I think I could have been really good at helping him crossover, but I guess it's not in the cards.

Anyway, I believe it is our job as humans to take care of each other as best we can, to uplift and encourage each other. That's how humanity survives, and if we're so lucky, that's how we thrive. If we can't care for humans, then let's care for animals, or plant life, or whatever. Just try to care for something more so than distrust, because we are all trying the best we can.

***
8.
WHAT CAN BOOK READERS SAY TO HELP YOU?

...I don't consider myself to be a writer at all. (Like I always say, if life had gone the way I wished it to go from when I was a little kid, I'd be an interior designer. I'd be a design star.) But, I'm just a normal person like anyone else, just trying to survive every day like everyone else in the world. Even though I cannot respond to emails and social media as much as I'd like to, I do read my Amazon reviews every so often, and I do gain a bit of excitement from each reader that comes from a place of consideration for the effort it takes to sit down a write down a story you feel compelled to tell even if it's unpopular topic. Of course, I absolutely love the five stars. They really encourage me to keep going.

***
9.
WHICH ADOPTION AGENCY DO YOU ADVOCATE FOR TODAY?

After studying and observing the intercountry adoption markets and being involved with people adopted from around the world and in the United States, we do not endorse any adoption agency. We recommend that you protect yourself before you transfer funds to a charity that permanently places and processes children. Before you know it the fees can run as high as $75,000 per child, starting with the bait of a cute irresistible photo, and a cheap and easy nonrefundable application fee to get you started. At least with foster care the child gets to keep his identity and retain access to biological family. (Excerpt from adoptiontruth.org).

***

10.
IS THERE A LAST MESSAGE YOU WANT TO GIVE TO READERS?

So glad I got to spend some time with you and share these stories. We might never meet, so I'm sending you good vibes, along with the wishes that you will be showered in your life with light, love, and abundance. Take care, my friend!

~Janine

GIVE YOURSELF A WRITING CHANCE

Hey, if you enjoyed this adventure or found any value in any information from this book, I'd be honored if you left a sentence or two at the online retailer. Comments can also be left on Amazon, Goodreads or the retailer's book description page.

I also invite you to investigate other books within the collection compiled by adult adoptees and titled Adoption Books for Adults. These books can be read in any order and consist of a variety of genres. Pick and choose your favorite type of book: memoir, anthology, or history and research. Keep in mind, these books are not the same type of stories you might hear intended for adopted children typically written by adoptive parents. Rather, this series has been garnered by the adoptive community—now adults. Because the adoption industry began as early as the 1600s, many adopted people have been placed overseas and are parents, aunts, uncles, grandparents, and even great grandparents today. As mentioned throughout the collective, many of us are seeking equal rights to our personal documents, such as adoption documents, citizenship, and birth certificates.

Finally, for healing and recovery, the last book I wrote is not specifically for adoptees, but can apply to anyone contending with surprises and the unknowns in life. Since I finished my own series, I hope help other non-writers with the process of sharing one's own story. Come on, when it comes to writing one's memoir, no one needs to be perfect. Everyone deserves to be heard!!

Stay updated here:

WEBSITES: Personal: janinevance.com
With sister: vancetwins.com | **Facebook Page:** Vance Twins
Adoption History: janinemyungja.com

SOCIAL: Facebook: Vance Twins
Goodreads: History & Anthologies: Janine Myung Ja
Philosophy & Personal Baggage: Janine Vance

Pssp: Remember to Review *Adoption Stories* on Amazon!
(It'll make Janine so happy to see your thoughts there!)
Adoption Books | Personal Books.

APPRECIATION

This series offers a short summary on what I've learned based on years of community engagement. I feel compelled to share these findings with you.

It is dedicated to all adopted people worldwide past, present, and future.

It is inspired by human rights organizations, particularly by indigenous and children's rights advocates.

I appreciate Patty Sang's proofreading eye.

I'm grateful for Michael Allen Potter's editorial expertise.

Special thanks to Roelie Post and Arun Dohle of Against Child Trafficking.

Without the loving support of my husband and daughters, these numerous years of reflection and research could never have happened.

Finally, if it were not for my sister's consistent excitement and encouragement, this book would not have been written.

Adoption Books for Adults
SERIES BY JANINE MYUNG JA

ACCIDENTS & RECOVERY

When you're hit by surprises sometimes you have to stop believing, and then begin again.

COMFORT CARE

The Power of Isolation & Going Back to Zen
These two ebooks are inside *Rise from the Dread* (paperback only)

KOREAN ADOPTEES WORLDWIDE

ADOPTION TRUTH & TRANSPARENCY WORLDWIDE NETWORK

Acknowledging the most ignored voices in adoption, yet the most vital when it comes to rights & protection.

A CRITIQUE ON ADOPTION

You don't have to be positive during a massacre. For those who were sent to a culture of saviorhood & advertised under the guise of love. Also a book promoting equal rights for recovering souls...